THE KROCKPOTS TO KASSEROLES

Easy Dinner with Mississippi Kween Cookbook

Caroline Sill

Legal & Disclaimer

The content and information in this book have been compiled from reliable resources, which are accurate based on the Author's knowledge, belief, expertise, and information. The Author cannot be held liable for any omissions and errors.

Acknowledgments

Creating a cookbook is a journey, and it wouldn't be possible without the support of so many wonderful people. First and foremost, I want to thank my family, whose love and encouragement have always been my greatest inspiration. To my friends who've tasted and tested these recipes, your feedback and enthusiasm have made this book even better.
I am deeply grateful to the editors and designers who brought these pages to life. Your hard work and creative vision turned this cookbook into something truly special.

A special thanks goes to my fellow home cooks who share their stories and recipes with the world. The joy of cooking is contagious, and you've all inspired me in ways you may never know. And, of course, to all of you, the readers, who make this cookbook meaningful. I hope it brings as much joy to your kitchen as it has to mine.

This book celebrates simple, delicious meals shared with the people we love. Thank you for letting me share your cooking adventures.

About the Author

As someone passionate about simplifying cooking for busy individuals and families, this cookbook was created with your everyday needs in mind. My mission is to provide practical, no-fuss recipes that bring joy to your table while saving you time and effort in the kitchen.

I understand how challenging it can be to juggle life's demands and still find time to make meals that are satisfying, nutritious, and family-approved. This cookbook is designed to take the stress out of mealtime, offering easy-to-follow recipes that fit seamlessly into your routine.

Whether you're managing a full household, prepping ahead for busy weeks, or just trying to enjoy homemade meals without spending hours in the kitchen, this book is here to help. Thank you for trusting me to be a part of your cooking journey—I'm honored to share these recipes with you and hope they bring as much joy to your home as they've brought to mine.

Table of Content

Introduction

Welcome to *Crockpots to Casseroles*

If there's one thing that makes life a little easier, it's having a meal that practically cooks itself. Welcome to *The Krockpots to Kasseroles*, where we bring you many mouthwatering recipes that prove you don't need to spend hours in the kitchen serving a delicious and comforting dish. This cookbook is all about embracing the beauty of slow cooking and one-pan meals—because who has time for complicated cooking when you've got a family to feed, a schedule to juggle, and life to live? Inside these pages, you'll find simple, hearty recipes that fit seamlessly into busy lives. Whether you're relying on your trusty slow cooker to bring dinner to life while running errands or whipping up a casserole packed with flavor and easy to throw together, we've got you covered. From comforting stews to spicy Cajun dishes and cheesy soups to vibrant pasta salads, each recipe is designed to save you time while still making your taste buds do a happy dance.

Here's what you can expect:

- **Crockpots**: Let your slow cooker do the heavy lifting. From tender meats to flavorful veggie stews, we've got dishes you can toss together in the morning and come home to a perfectly cooked meal.
- **Casseroles**: The ultimate one-dish wonders. These casseroles are easy to prep, easy to clean up, and even easier to enjoy. They're filling, comforting, and perfect for feeding a crowd—or your hungry family.

We believe that good food doesn't have to be complicated, and with these recipes, you'll spend less time stressing in the kitchen and more time enjoying the company of your loved ones. So grab your apron, fire up that slow cooker, or preheat that oven, and let's get cooking. Because with *Krockpots to Kasseroles*, every meal is a chance to bring a little joy to your table—without the fuss.

Wake-Up Wonders

Slow Cooker Cinnamon Roll Casserole

Serves	1	**Prep Time**	10 Minute	
		Cook Time	3 Hours	

- 1/2 can cinnamon rolls, cut into small pieces
- 1/4 cup milk
- 1/4 cup heavy cream
- 1/4 cup brown sugar
- 1/2 teaspoon cinnamon
- 1/4 teaspoon vanilla extract
- 1 tablespoon butter, melted
- 1/4 cup cream cheese, softened
- 1/4 cup powdered sugar

Instructions

1. Grease the slow cooker and add cinnamon roll pieces.
2. In a bowl, whisk together milk, heavy cream, brown sugar, cinnamon, vanilla extract, and melted butter. Pour over the cinnamon rolls.
3. Cook on low for 3 hours, until golden and bubbly.
4. Mix cream cheese with powdered sugar to create a glaze, then drizzle over the casserole before serving.

Crockpot Sausage and Egg Breakfast Casserole

Serves 1

Prep Time 10 MInute

Cook Time 3 Hours

- 1/2 cup cooked sausage, crumbled
- 1/4 cup bell pepper, diced
- 1/4 cup onion, diced
- 1/4 cup shredded cheddar cheese
- 1/2 cup eggs, beaten
- 1/4 cup milk
- Salt and pepper to taste

Instructions

1. Grease the slow cooker and layer cooked sausage, bell pepper, onion, and cheddar cheese.
2. In a bowl, whisk together eggs, milk, salt, and pepper. Pour over the sausage mixture.
3. Cook on low for 3 hours until eggs are fully set.
4. Serve warm with extra cheese if desired.

Slow Cooker Banana Nut Oatmeal

Serves	1	Prep Time	5 Minute	Cook Time	3 Hours

- 1/2 cup rolled oats
- 1/4 cup banana, sliced
- 1 tablespoon chopped walnuts
- 1/4 cup almond milk
- 1/4 cup water
- 1 tablespoon brown sugar
- 1/4 teaspoon cinnamon

Instructions

1. Add rolled oats, banana slices, walnuts, almond milk, water, brown sugar, and cinnamon to the slow cooker.
2. Stir to combine, then cook on low for 3 hours, stirring halfway through.
3. Serve hot with additional banana slices or nuts as a topping.

Crockpot Apple Cinnamon Quinoa

Serves	1		**Prep Time**	**5** Minute		**Cook Time**	**3** Hours

- 1/2 cup quinoa, rinsed
- 1/2 apple, diced
- 1/4 cup almond milk
- 1/4 cup water
- 1/2 teaspoon cinnamon
- 1 tablespoon maple syrup
- 1 tablespoon chopped pecans

Instructions

1. Combine quinoa, apple, almond milk, water, cinnamon, and maple syrup in the slow cooker.
2. Stir to combine and cook on low for 3 hours.
3. Top with chopped pecans and serve hot.

Slow Cooker Breakfast Casserole with Bacon and Potatoes

	Serves	1		Prep Time	10 Minute		Cook Time	4 Hours

- 1/2 cup cooked bacon, crumbled
- 1/2 cup diced potatoes
- 1/4 cup bell pepper, diced
- 1/4 cup onion, diced

- 1/4 cup shredded cheddar cheese
- 1/2 cup eggs, beaten
- 1/4 cup milk
- Salt and pepper to taste

Instructions

1. Grease the slow cooker and layer crumbled bacon, diced potatoes, bell pepper, onion, and cheddar cheese.
2. In a bowl, whisk together eggs, milk, salt, and pepper, then pour over the mixture.
3. Cook on low for 4 hours, until eggs are fully set and potatoes are tender.
4. Serve warm with extra cheese if desired.

Crockpot Blueberry French Toast Casserole

Serves	1	Prep Time	10 Minute	Cook Time	3 Hours

- 1/2 loaf French bread, cut into cubes
- 1/4 cup blueberries (fresh or frozen)
- 1/4 cup eggs, beaten
- 1/4 cup milk
- 1/4 cup heavy cream
- 1 tablespoon maple syrup
- 1/2 teaspoon cinnamon
- 1/4 teaspoon vanilla extract

Instructions

1. Grease the slow cooker and layer the French bread cubes with blueberries.
2. In a bowl, whisk together eggs, milk, heavy cream, maple syrup, cinnamon, and vanilla extract. Pour over the bread and blueberries.
3. Cook on low for 3 hours until the casserole is set and golden.
4. Serve with extra maple syrup if desired.

Slow Cooker Sweet Potato Breakfast Hash

	Serves	1		Prep Time	10 Minute		Cook Time	4 Hours

- 1/2 cup sweet potatoes, diced
- 1/4 cup bell pepper, diced
- 1/4 cup onion, diced
- 1/4 cup cooked sausage, crumbled
- 1/4 cup eggs, beaten
- Salt and pepper to taste

Instructions

1. Add diced sweet potatoes, bell pepper, onion, and crumbled sausage to the slow cooker.
2. Pour eggs over the mixture, add salt and pepper, and stir gently to combine.
3. Cook on low for 4 hours, stirring occasionally, until sweet potatoes are tender.
4. Serve warm with a side of avocado or salsa.

Crockpot Egg and Veggie Frittata

| | Serves | 1 | | Prep Time | 10 Minute | | Cook Time | 3 Hours |

- 1/2 cup mushrooms, sliced
- 1/4 cup spinach, chopped
- 1/4 cup bell pepper, diced
- 1/2 cup eggs, beaten
- 1/4 cup milk
- 1/4 cup feta cheese, crumbled
- Salt and pepper to taste

Instructions

1. Grease the slow cooker and add mushrooms, spinach, and bell pepper.
2. In a bowl, whisk together eggs, milk, feta cheese, salt, and pepper. Pour over the veggies.
3. Cook on low for 3 hours until the eggs are set and the frittata is golden.
4. Serve warm with a sprinkle of extra cheese.

Slow Cooker Chocolate Peanut Butter Oatmeal

🍴 Serves	1	Prep Time	5 MInute	Cook Time	3 Hours

- 1/2 cup rolled oats
- 1 tablespoon peanut butter
- 1 tablespoon cocoa powder
- 1/4 cup almond milk
- 1/4 cup water
- 1 tablespoon honey
- 1/4 teaspoon vanilla extract

Instructions

1. Add oats, peanut butter, cocoa powder, almond milk, water, honey, and vanilla extract to the slow cooker.
2. Stir to combine and cook on low for 3 hours, stirring halfway through.
3. Serve hot with extra peanut butter or chocolate chips on top.

Crockpot Chia Pudding Breakfast

Serves 1   **Prep Time** 5 Minute   **Cook Time** 3 Hours

- 1/2 cup chia seeds
- 1/4 cup almond milk
- 1/4 cup coconut milk
- 1 tablespoon honey
- 1/4 teaspoon vanilla extract
- Fresh berries for topping

Instructions

1. Add chia seeds, almond milk, coconut milk, honey, and vanilla extract to the slow cooker.
2. Stir to combine and cook on low for 3 hours until the mixture thickens into a pudding.
3. Top with fresh berries and serve warm or chilled.

One-Pot Magic

Slow Cooker Chicken and Dumplings

Serves	1	Prep Time	10 Minute	Cook Time	6 Hours

- 1 small chicken breast
- 1/4 cup carrots, sliced
- 1/4 cup celery, chopped
- 1/4 cup frozen peas
- 1 can cream of chicken soup
- 1/2 cup chicken broth
- 1/2 teaspoon garlic powder
- 1/4 teaspoon black pepper
- 1/4 cup biscuit mix

Instructions

1. Add chicken, carrots, celery, peas, soup, and chicken broth to the slow cooker.
2. Stir in garlic powder and black pepper.
3. Cover and cook on low for 6 hours.
4. Before serving, mix in biscuit mix, forming small dumplings over the top.
5. Cover and cook for an additional 30 minutes until dumplings are cooked through.

Crockpot Beef Stroganoff

| Serves | 1 | Prep Time | 10 Minute | Cook Time | 7 Hours |

- 4 ounces of beef stew meat
- 1/4 small onion, diced
- 1/4 cup beef broth
- 1/4 teaspoon garlic powder
- 1/2 teaspoon paprika
- 1/4 cup sour cream
- 1/4 cup cream cheese, cubed
- 1/4 cup egg noodles

Instructions

1. Place beef, onion, beef broth, garlic powder, and paprika in the crockpot.
2. Stir to combine and cook on low for 7 hours.
3. About 30 minutes before serving, add egg noodles and stir in sour cream and cream cheese.
4. Continue cooking for 30 more minutes until noodles are tender.

Slow Cooker BBQ Pulled Pork

![] Serves	1	Prep Time	5 Minute	Cook Time	8 Hours

- 4 ounces pork shoulder
- 1/4 cup BBQ sauce
- 2 tablespoons chicken broth
- 1 small onion, sliced
- 1/4 teaspoon smoked paprika

Instructions

1. Place pork, BBQ sauce, chicken broth, onion, and paprika into the slow cooker.
2. Stir to coat the pork evenly.
3. Cover and cook on low for 8 hours.
4. Shred the pork with a fork and serve on a small bun or over rice.

Crockpot Lemon Garlic Chicken

| | Serves | 1 | | Prep Time | 10 Minute | | Cook Time | 6 Hours |

- 1 small chicken breast
- 1/4 teaspoon garlic powder
- 1/4 teaspoon lemon zest
- 1 tablespoon lemon juice
- 1/4 cup chicken broth
- 1 tablespoon olive oil
- Salt and pepper to taste

Instructions

1. Season the chicken with garlic powder, lemon zest, salt, and pepper.
2. Place chicken in the crockpot and pour lemon juice, olive oil, and chicken broth over it.
3. Cover and cook on low for 6 hours.
4. Serve with a side of rice or roasted vegetables.

Slow Cooker Vegetable Curry

Serves	1	
Prep Time	10 Minute	
Cook Time	6 Hours	

- 1/2 cup cauliflower florets
- 1/2 cup chopped carrots
- 1/4 cup diced onion
- 1/4 cup diced tomatoes
- 1/2 cup coconut milk
- 1 tablespoon curry powder
- 1/4 teaspoon garlic powder
- Salt to taste

Instructions

1. Add all vegetables, tomatoes, coconut milk, curry powder, garlic powder, and salt to the slow cooker.
2. Stir to combine.
3. Cover and cook on low for 6 hours.
4. Serve over rice or enjoy as is.

Crockpot Italian Meatballs

	Serves	1		Prep Time	10 Minute		Cook Time	7 Hours

- 4 small meatballs (store-bought or homemade)
- 1/4 cup marinara sauce
- 1/4 cup shredded mozzarella cheese

Instructions

1. Place meatballs in the crockpot and cover with marinara sauce.
2. Cover and cook on low for 7 hours.
3. About 10 minutes before serving, sprinkle mozzarella cheese over the meatballs and let it melt.
4. Serve on pasta or as a sandwich.

Slow Cooker Chicken Fajitas

Serves	1	Prep Time	5 Minute	Cook Time	6 Hours

- 1 small chicken breast, sliced
- 1/4 small bell pepper, sliced
- 1/4 small onion, sliced
- 1 tablespoon fajita seasoning
- 1/4 cup chicken broth
- 1 small tortilla (optional)

Instructions

1. Combine chicken, bell pepper, onion, fajita seasoning, and chicken broth in the slow cooker.
2. Stir to coat evenly and cover.
3. Cook on low for 6 hours.
4. Serve with a warm tortilla or over rice.

Crockpot Beef and Potato Casserole

| Serves | 1 | | Prep Time | 10 Minute | | Cook Time | 7 Hours |

- 4 ounces ground beef
- 1 small potato, sliced
- 1/4 cup shredded cheddar cheese
- 1/4 cup beef broth
- 1/4 teaspoon garlic powder

Instructions

1. Brown the ground beef and drain the fat.
2. Layer sliced potatoes, beef, garlic powder, and beef broth in the crockpot.
3. Cover and cook on low for 7 hours.
4. Sprinkle shredded cheese over the casserole during the last 10 minutes of cooking.

Slow Cooker Chili Mac

	Serves	1		Prep Time	10 Minute		Cook Time	6 Hours

- 4 ounces ground beef
- 1/4 cup elbow macaroni
- 1/4 cup diced tomatoes
- 1/4 cup kidney beans, drained and rinsed
- 1/4 cup cheddar cheese
- 1/4 teaspoon chilli powder

Instructions

1. Brown the ground beef in a pan and drain any excess fat.
2. Add beef, macaroni, diced tomatoes, kidney beans, and chilli powder to the slow cooker.
3. Stir to combine and cover.
4. Cook on low for 6 hours.
5. Sprinkle with cheddar cheese just before serving.

Crockpot Chicken Parmesan

| | Serves | 1 | | Prep Time | 10 Minute | | Cook Time | 6 Hours |

- 1 small chicken breast
- 1/4 cup marinara sauce
- 1/4 cup shredded mozzarella cheese
- 1 tablespoon grated Parmesan cheese

Instructions

1. Place the chicken breast in the crockpot and cover with marinara sauce.
2. Cook on low for 6 hours.
3. Top the chicken with mozzarella and Parmesan cheese 10 minutes before serving.
4. Serve with pasta or a side salad.

Souped-Up Seasons

Slow Cooker Spicy Chicken Tortilla Soup

| Serves | 1 | Prep Time | 10 Minute | Cook Time | 6 Hours |

- 1 small chicken breast, diced
- 1/4 cup onion, chopped
- 1/4 cup bell pepper, chopped
- 1/4 cup corn kernels (fresh or frozen)
- 1/2 cup diced tomatoes
- 1/4 teaspoon chilli powder
- 1/4 teaspoon cumin
- 1/4 teaspoon garlic powder
- 1/2 cup chicken broth
- 1/4 cup tortilla chips, crushed
- Salt and pepper to taste

Instructions

1. Add diced chicken, onion, bell pepper, corn, diced tomatoes, chilli powder, cumin, garlic powder, chicken broth, salt, and pepper to the slow cooker.
2. Stir to combine and cook on low for 6 hours.
3. Before serving, stir in crushed tortilla chips for a crunchy texture and extra flavour.

Crockpot Creamy Mushroom Soup

| | Serves | 1 | | Prep Time | 10 Minute | | Cook Time | 6 Hours |

- 1/4 cup mushrooms, sliced
- 1/4 cup onion, chopped
- 1/4 cup celery, chopped
- 1/4 teaspoon thyme
- 1/4 teaspoon garlic powder
- 1/2 cup vegetable broth
- 1/4 cup heavy cream
- Salt and pepper to taste

Instructions

1. Place mushrooms, onion, celery, thyme, garlic powder, vegetable broth, salt, and pepper into the crockpot.
2. Stir to combine and cook on low for 6 hours.
3. After cooking, stir in the heavy cream and serve warm.

Slow Cooker Sweet Potato and Carrot Soup

	Serves	1		Prep Time	10 Minute		Cook Time	6 Hours

- 1 small sweet potato, peeled and cubed
- 1/4 cup carrots, chopped
- 1/4 small onion, chopped
- 1/4 teaspoon cinnamon
- 1/4 teaspoon garlic powder
- 1/2 cup vegetable broth
- 1/4 cup coconut milk
- Salt and pepper to taste

Instructions

1. Add sweet potato, carrots, onion, cinnamon, garlic powder, vegetable broth, salt, and pepper to the slow cooker.
2. Stir to combine and cook on low for 6 hours.
3. Use an immersion blender to blend until smooth, then stir in coconut milk before serving.

Crockpot Beef and Vegetable Stew

Serves	1	**Prep Time**	10 Minute	**Cook Time**	7 Hours

- 4 ounces of beef stew meat, cubed
- 1/4 cup carrots, chopped
- 1/4 cup potatoes, diced
- 1/4 cup green beans, chopped
- 1/2 cup beef broth
- 1/4 teaspoon garlic powder
- 1/4 teaspoon thyme
- Salt and pepper to taste

Instructions

1. Place beef stew meat, carrots, potatoes, green beans, garlic powder, thyme, beef broth, salt, and pepper into the crockpot.
2. Stir well, cover, and cook on low for 7 hours.
3. Stir before serving and season with additional salt and pepper if needed.

Slow Cooker Chicken and Rice Soup

	Serves	1		Prep Time	10 Minute		Cook Time	6 Hours

- 1 small chicken breast, diced
- 1/4 cup carrots, chopped
- 1/4 cup celery, chopped
- 1/4 cup onion, chopped
- 1/4 cup cooked rice
- 1/2 cup chicken broth
- 1/4 teaspoon thyme
- Salt and pepper to taste

Instructions

1. Add chicken, carrots, celery, onion, chicken broth, and thyme to the slow cooker.
2. Stir to combine and cook on low for 6 hours.
3. Before serving, stir in the cooked rice and season with salt and pepper to taste.

Crockpot Tomato Basil Soup

	Serves	1		Prep Time	5 Minute		Cook Time	6 Hours

- 1/2 cup crushed tomatoes
- 1/4 cup tomato sauce
- 1/2 cup vegetable broth
- 1/4 teaspoon garlic powder
- 1/4 teaspoon dried basil
- Salt and pepper to taste
- 1/4 cup heavy cream

Instructions

1. Place crushed tomatoes, tomato sauce, vegetable broth, garlic powder, basil, salt, and pepper in the crockpot.
2. Stir to combine and cook on low for 6 hours.
3. Stir in heavy cream before serving for a rich and creamy texture.

Slow Cooker Spicy Lentil Soup

Serves	1	**Prep Time**	10 Minute	**Cook Time**	6 Hours		

- 1/4 cup dry lentils
- 1/4 cup carrots, chopped
- 1/4 cup onion, chopped
- 1/4 teaspoon cumin
- 1/4 teaspoon chilli powder
- 1/2 cup vegetable broth
- 1/4 teaspoon garlic powder
- Salt and pepper to taste

Instructions

1. Add lentils, carrots, onion, cumin, chilli powder, garlic powder, vegetable broth, salt, and pepper to the slow cooker.
2. Stir to combine and cook on low for 6 hours.
3. Adjust seasoning with salt and pepper before serving.

Crockpot Creamy Broccoli Cheddar Soup

Serves	1	Prep Time	10 Minute	Cook Time	6 Hours

- 1/4 cup broccoli florets
- 1/4 cup onion, chopped
- 1/4 cup carrots, chopped
- 1/2 cup chicken broth

- 1/4 cup heavy cream
- 1/4 cup shredded cheddar cheese
- Salt and pepper to taste

Instructions

1. Add broccoli, onion, carrots, chicken broth, salt, and pepper to the crockpot.
2. Stir and cook on low for 6 hours, until vegetables are tender.
3. Stir in heavy cream and cheddar cheese before serving.

Slow Cooker Sweet Corn Chowder

| Serves | 1 | | Prep Time | 10 Minute | | Cook Time | 6 Hours |

- 1/4 cup corn kernels (fresh or frozen)
- 1/4 cup potatoes, diced
- 1/4 cup onion, chopped
- 1/4 teaspoon garlic powder
- 1/2 cup vegetable broth
- 1/4 cup heavy cream
- Salt and pepper to taste

Instructions

1. Combine corn, potatoes, onion, garlic powder, vegetable broth, salt, and pepper in the slow cooker.
2. Stir to combine and cook on low for 6 hours.
3. Add heavy cream before serving for a creamy, comforting texture.

Crockpot Chili Soup

Serves 1 | **Prep Time** 10 Minute | **Cook Time** 6 Hours

- 1/4 cup ground beef or turkey, browned
- 1/4 cup kidney beans, drained and rinsed
- 1/4 cup diced tomatoes
- 1/4 cup onion, chopped
- 1/4 teaspoon chilli powder
- 1/4 teaspoon cumin
- 1/2 cup beef or chicken broth
- Salt and pepper to taste

Instructions

1. Add ground beef or turkey, kidney beans, diced tomatoes, onion, chilli powder, cumin, beef or chicken broth, salt, and pepper to the crockpot.
2. Stir to combine and cook on low for 6 hours.
3. Serve hot with a dollop of sour cream or shredded cheese.

Satisfying Pasta Salad Dishes

Slow Cooker Italian Pasta Salad

Serves	1		Prep Time	10 Minute		Cook Time	2 Hours

- 1/2 cup rotini pasta, cooked and drained
- 1/4 cup cherry tomatoes, halved
- 1/4 cup black olives, sliced
- 1/4 cup mozzarella cheese, cubed
- 2 tablespoons Italian dressing
- 1 tablespoon olive oil
- 1/4 teaspoon oregano
- Salt and pepper to taste

Instructions

1. Combine cooked pasta, cherry tomatoes, olives, mozzarella cheese, Italian dressing, olive oil, oregano, salt, and pepper in the slow cooker.
2. Stir gently to combine, then cook on low for 2 hours to allow flavours to meld together.
3. Serve chilled or at room temperature.

Crockpot Mediterranean Pasta Salad

	Serves	1		Prep Time	10 Minute		Cook Time	2 Hours

- 1/2 cup penne pasta, cooked and drained
- 1/4 cup cucumber, chopped
- 1/4 cup feta cheese, crumbled
- 1/4 cup kalamata olives, sliced
- 2 tablespoons red onion, finely chopped
- 2 tablespoons olive oil
- 1 tablespoon lemon juice
- 1/4 teaspoon dried oregano
- Salt and pepper to taste

Instructions

1. In the slow cooker, mix the cooked penne pasta, cucumber, feta cheese, kalamata olives, red onion, olive oil, lemon juice, oregano, salt, and pepper.
2. Stir gently and cook on low for 2 hours to let the flavours blend.
3. Serve chilled or at room temperature.

Slow Cooker Bacon Ranch Pasta Salad

| Serves | 1 | Prep Time | 10 Minute | Cook Time | 2 Hours |

- 1/2 cup elbow macaroni, cooked and drained
- 1/4 cup cooked bacon, crumbled
- 1/4 cup shredded cheddar cheese
- 2 tablespoons ranch dressing
- 2 tablespoons sour cream
- 1 tablespoon green onions, chopped
- Salt and pepper to taste

Instructions

1. Combine cooked elbow macaroni, bacon, cheddar cheese, ranch dressing, sour cream, green onions, salt, and pepper in the slow cooker.
2. Stir gently to combine and cook on low for 2 hours.
3. Serve chilled for a creamy, savoury pasta salad.

Crockpot Southwest Pasta Salad

Serves 1 **Prep Time** 10 Minute **Cook Time** 2 Hours

- 1/2 cup bowtie pasta, cooked and drained
- 1/4 cup corn kernels (fresh or frozen)
- 1/4 cup black beans, drained and rinsed
- 1/4 cup red bell pepper, chopped
- 1/4 teaspoon cumin
- 1 tablespoon lime juice
- 2 tablespoons cilantro, chopped
- 1/4 cup salsa
- Salt and pepper to taste

Instructions

1. In the slow cooker, mix the cooked bowtie pasta, corn, black beans, red bell pepper, cumin, lime juice, cilantro, salsa, salt, and pepper.
2. Stir to combine and cook on low for 2 hours.
3. Serve chilled with a sprinkle of additional cilantro for garnish.

Slow Cooker Caprese Pasta Salad

Serves 1   **Prep Time** 10 Minute   **Cook Time** 2 Hours

- 1/2 cup rotini pasta, cooked and drained
- 1/4 cup cherry tomatoes, halved
- 1/4 cup fresh mozzarella balls, halved
- 2 tablespoons balsamic vinegar
- 1 tablespoon olive oil
- 1/4 teaspoon dried basil
- Salt and pepper to taste

Instructions

1. Combine the cooked rotini pasta, cherry tomatoes, mozzarella balls, balsamic vinegar, olive oil, basil, salt, and pepper in the slow cooker.
2. Stir gently to combine and cook on low for 2 hours.
3. Serve chilled or at room temperature, topped with extra basil for garnish.

Crockpot Pesto Pasta Salad

	Serves	1		Prep Time	10 Minute		Cook Time	2 Hours

- 1/2 cup fusilli pasta, cooked and drained
- 2 tablespoons pesto sauce
- 1/4 cup cherry tomatoes, halved
- 1/4 cup mozzarella cheese, cubed
- 2 tablespoons Parmesan cheese, grated
- Salt and pepper to taste

Instructions

1. Toss the cooked fusilli pasta, pesto sauce, cherry tomatoes, mozzarella, Parmesan cheese, salt, and pepper in the slow cooker.
2. Stir to combine and cook on low for 2 hours.
3. Serve chilled for a fresh and vibrant flavour.

Slow Cooker Chicken Caesar Pasta Salad

Serves	Prep Time	Cook Time
1	10 Minute	2 Hours

- 1/2 cup rotini pasta, cooked and drained
- 1/4 cup cooked chicken breast, chopped
- 2 tablespoons Caesar dressing
- 2 tablespoons grated Parmesan cheese
- 1/4 cup croutons
- Salt and pepper to taste

Instructions

1. Combine cooked rotini pasta, chopped chicken, Caesar dressing, Parmesan cheese, croutons, salt, and pepper in the slow cooker.
2. Stir to mix well and cook on low for 2 hours.
3. Serve chilled with a sprinkle of extra Parmesan cheese.

Crockpot Asian Sesame Pasta Salad

| Serves | 1 | Prep Time | 10 Minute | Cook Time | 2 Hours |

- 1/2 cup spaghetti, cooked and drained
- 1/4 cup shredded carrots
- 1/4 cup cucumber, julienned
- 2 tablespoons sesame oil
- 1 tablespoon soy sauce
- 1 tablespoon rice vinegar
- 1/4 teaspoon ginger
- 1 tablespoon sesame seeds
- Salt and pepper to taste

Instructions

1. In the slow cooker, combine cooked spaghetti, shredded carrots, cucumber, sesame oil, soy sauce, rice vinegar, ginger, sesame seeds, salt, and pepper.
2. Stir to combine and cook on low for 2 hours.
3. Serve chilled, garnished with additional sesame seeds.

Slow Cooker Greek Pasta Salad

	Serves	1		Prep Time	10 Minute		Cook Time	2 Hours

- 1/2 cup rotini pasta, cooked and drained
- 1/4 cup Kalamata olives, sliced
- 1/4 cup cucumber, diced
- 1/4 cup red onion, finely chopped
- 1/4 cup feta cheese, crumbled
- 2 tablespoons olive oil
- 1 tablespoon lemon juice
- 1/4 teaspoon oregano
- Salt and pepper to taste

Instructions

1. Combine cooked rotini pasta, Kalamata olives, cucumber, red onion, feta cheese, olive oil, lemon juice, oregano, salt, and pepper in the slow cooker.
2. Stir to combine and cook on low for 2 hours.
3. Serve chilled or at room temperature for a refreshing side.

Crockpot Avocado Pasta Salad

| Serves | 1 | Prep Time | 10 Minute | Cook Time | 2 Hours |

- 1/2 cup farfalle pasta, cooked and drained
- 1/4 cup avocado, diced
- 1/4 cup cherry tomatoes, halved
- 2 tablespoons lime juice
- 1/4 teaspoon cumin
- Salt and pepper to taste

Instructions

1. Mix the cooked farfalle pasta, diced avocado, cherry tomatoes, lime juice, cumin, salt, and pepper in the slow cooker.
2. Stir to combine and cook on low for 2 hours.
3. Serve chilled with a drizzle of extra lime juice.

Casserole Comforts

Slow Cooker Chicken Alfredo Casserole

| Serves | 1 | | Prep Time | 10 Minute | | Cook Time | 3 Hours |

- 1/2 cup cooked chicken breast, shredded
- 1/2 cup rotini pasta, uncooked
- 1/4 cup Parmesan cheese, grated
- 1/4 cup mozzarella cheese, shredded
- 1/2 cup Alfredo sauce
- 1/4 cup milk
- 1/4 teaspoon garlic powder
- Salt and pepper to taste

Instructions

1. In the slow cooker, combine shredded chicken, uncooked rotini pasta, Parmesan cheese, mozzarella cheese, Alfredo sauce, milk, garlic powder, salt, and pepper.
2. Stir gently to combine, then cook on low for 3 hours or until pasta is tender.
3. Serve warm with a sprinkle of extra Parmesan cheese.

Crockpot Cheesy Broccoli Rice Casserole

Serves	1	Prep Time	10 Minute	Cook Time	3 Hours

- 1/2 cup cooked rice
- 1/4 cup frozen broccoli florets
- 1/2 cup cheddar cheese, shredded
- 1/4 cup sour cream
- 1/4 cup chicken broth
- 1/4 teaspoon garlic powder
- Salt and pepper to taste

Instructions

1. In the slow cooker, combine cooked rice, frozen broccoli, cheddar cheese, sour cream, chicken broth, garlic powder, salt, and pepper.
2. Stir gently, then cook on low for 3 hours, stirring once or twice during cooking.
3. Serve hot as a comforting side dish.

Slow Cooker Beef and Potato Casserole

Serves	1	**Prep Time**	15 Minute	**Cook Time**	4 Hours

- 1/2 cup ground beef, cooked and drained
- 1/2 cup potatoes, thinly sliced
- 1/4 cup onion, diced
- 1/4 cup sour cream
- 1/4 cup cheddar cheese, shredded
- 1/4 cup beef broth
- 1/4 teaspoon thyme
- Salt and pepper to taste

Instructions

1. Layer the slow cooker with ground beef, sliced potatoes, and diced onion.
2. Mix sour cream, cheddar cheese, beef broth, thyme, salt, and pepper, then pour over the beef and potatoes.
3. Cook on low for 4 hours or until potatoes are tender and the casserole is bubbly.

Crockpot Chicken and Spinach Casserole

Serves 1	**Prep Time** 10 Minute	**Cook Time** 3 Hours

- 1/2 cup cooked chicken breast, diced
- 1/4 cup spinach, chopped
- 1/2 cup cream cheese
- 1/4 cup Parmesan cheese, grated
- 1/4 cup mozzarella cheese, shredded
- 1/4 cup chicken broth
- 1/4 teaspoon garlic powder
- Salt and pepper to taste

Instructions

1. In the slow cooker, combine diced chicken, chopped spinach, cream cheese, Parmesan cheese, mozzarella cheese, chicken broth, garlic powder, salt, and pepper.
2. Stir gently to combine, then cook on low for 3 hours, stirring halfway through.
3. Serve warm with a side of crusty bread.

Slow Cooker Mac and Cheese Casserole

| Serves | 1 | | Prep Time | 10 Minute | | Cook Time | 3 Hours |

- 1/2 cup elbow macaroni, uncooked
- 1/4 cup cheddar cheese, shredded
- 1/4 cup mozzarella cheese, shredded
- 1/4 cup milk
- 1/4 cup heavy cream
- 1 tablespoon butter
- 1/4 teaspoon mustard powder
- Salt and pepper to taste

Instructions

1. Combine uncooked macaroni, cheddar cheese, mozzarella cheese, milk, heavy cream, butter, mustard powder, salt, and pepper in the slow cooker.
2. Stir gently, then cook on low for 3 hours, stirring occasionally.
3. Serve hot and creamy with a sprinkle of extra cheese.

Crockpot Sweet Potato and Sausage Casserole

Serves 1 | **Prep Time** 10 Minute | **Cook Time** 4 Hours

- 1/2 cup sweet potatoes, cubed
- 1/2 cup cooked sausage, crumbled
- 1/4 cup onion, diced
- 1/4 cup cheddar cheese, shredded
- 1/4 cup sour cream
- 1/4 cup chicken broth
- 1/4 teaspoon paprika
- Salt and pepper to taste

Instructions

1. In the slow cooker, combine sweet potatoes, crumbled sausage, diced onion, cheddar cheese, sour cream, chicken broth, paprika, salt, and pepper.
2. Stir to mix, then cook on low for 4 hours or until sweet potatoes are tender.
3. Serve warm as a hearty main dish or side.

Slow Cooker Tuna Noodle Casserole

	Serves	1		Prep Time	10 Minute		Cook Time	3 Hours

- 1/2 cup egg noodles, uncooked
- 1/4 cup canned tuna, drained
- 1/4 cup peas, frozen
- 1/4 cup cream of mushroom soup
- 1/4 cup cheddar cheese, shredded
- 1/4 cup milk
- Salt and pepper to taste

Instructions

1. In the slow cooker, combine uncooked egg noodles, canned tuna, peas, cream of mushroom soup, cheddar cheese, milk, salt, and pepper.
2. Stir gently to combine, then cook on low for 3 hours, stirring occasionally.
3. Serve hot with extra cheese if desired.

Crockpot Stuffing and Sausage Casserole

| | Serves | 1 | | Prep Time | 10 Minute | | Cook Time | 3 Hours |

- 1/2 cup stuffing mix
- 1/2 cup cooked sausage, crumbled
- 1/4 cup celery, chopped
- 1/4 cup onion, diced
- 1/4 cup chicken broth
- 1/4 teaspoon sage
- Salt and pepper to taste

Instructions

1. In the slow cooker, combine the stuffing mix, crumbled sausage, chopped celery, diced onion, chicken broth, sage, salt, and pepper.
2. Stir gently to combine, then cook on low for 3 hours, stirring halfway through.
3. Serve warm as a savoury side dish or main course.

Slow Cooker Beef Stroganoff Casserole

| Serves | 1 | Prep Time | 10 Minute | Cook Time | 3 Hours |

- 1/2 cup egg noodles, uncooked
- 1/4 cup beef stew meat, browned
- 1/4 cup sour cream
- 1/4 cup beef broth
- 1/4 cup onion, diced
- 1/4 teaspoon paprika
- Salt and pepper to taste

Instructions

1. In the slow cooker, combine uncooked egg noodles, browned beef stew meat, sour cream, beef broth, diced onion, paprika, salt, and pepper.
2. Stir gently, then cook on low for 3 hours, stirring occasionally.
3. Serve hot with extra sour cream for creaminess.

Crockpot Veggie and Rice Casserole

Serves	1	Prep Time	10 Minute
		Cook Time	3 Hours

- 1/2 cup cooked rice
- 1/4 cup mixed vegetables (carrots, peas, corn)
- 1/4 cup cream of mushroom soup
- 1/4 cup cheddar cheese, shredded
- 1/4 cup milk
- Salt and pepper to taste

Instructions

1. In the slow cooker, combine cooked rice, mixed vegetables, cream of mushroom soup, cheddar cheese, milk, salt, and pepper.
2. Stir to mix, then cook on low for 3 hours, stirring occasionally.
3. Serve warm as a simple, comforting side dish.

Conclusion

And there you have it—lots of recipes to simplify your meals, brighten your table, and bring your family together without the stress. *The Krockpots to Kasseroles* prove that great food doesn't need to be complicated, from slow-cooked, fall-apart tender dishes to casseroles that practically make themselves. Whether you're feeding a crowd, just yourself, or looking for something cozy or a bit more adventurous, there's a recipe here for every craving and schedule.

By now, you've got a collection of go-to meals that make weeknight dinners, weekend get-togethers, and everything in between much easier and more delicious. The beauty of these recipes is their simplicity—easy prep, minimal fuss, and maximum flavor. You don't have to be a professional chef to cook like one. Just toss ingredients into your slow cooker or mix up a casserole, and let the magic happen.

As you flip through these pages, I hope you enjoy the process of cooking just as much as the end result. The best meals aren't just about the food—they're about the memories you make, the people you share them with, and the joy of sitting down to something that tastes as good as it feels.
Here's to effortless meals, endless flavor, and a little more time to enjoy the things that matter most. Happy cooking!

14-Day Meal Planner

DAILY MEAL PLANNER — DAY 1

DATE:

BREAKFAST

....
....
....
....

LUNCH

....
....
....
....

DINNER

....
....
....
....

SNACK

....
....
....
....

NOTE

....
....
....
....

DAILY MEAL PLANNER

DAY 2

DATE:

BREAKFAST

....
....
....
....

LUNCH

....
....
....
....

DINNER

....
....
....
....

SNACK

....
....
....
....

NOTE

....
....
....
....

DAILY MEAL PLANNER

DAY 3

DATE:

BREAKFAST

....
....
....
....

LUNCH

....
....
....
....

DINNER

....
....
....
....

SNACK

....
....
....
....

NOTE

....
....
....
....

DAILY MEAL PLANNER

DAY 4

DATE:

BREAKFAST

....
....
....
....

LUNCH

....
....
....
....

DINNER

....
....
....
....

SNACK

....
....
....
....

NOTE

....
....
....
....

DAILY MEAL PLANNER

DAY 5

DATE:

BREAKFAST

....
....
....
....

LUNCH

....
....
....
....

DINNER

....
....
....
....

SNACK

....
....
....
....

NOTE

....
....
....
....

DAILY MEAL PLANNER

DAY 6

DATE:

BREAKFAST

....
....
....
....

LUNCH

....
....
....
....

DINNER

....
....
....
....

SNACK

....
....
....
....

NOTE

....
....
....
....

DAILY MEAL PLANNER

DAY 7

DATE:

BREAKFAST

....
....
....
....

LUNCH

....
....
....
....

DINNER

....
....
....
....

SNACK

....
....
....
....

NOTE

....
....
....
....

DAILY MEAL PLANNER

DAY 8

DATE:

BREAKFAST

....
....
....
....

LUNCH

....
....
....
....

DINNER

....
....
....
....

SNACK

....
....
....
....

NOTE

....
....
....
....

DAILY MEAL PLANNER

DAY 9

DATE:

BREAKFAST

....
....
....
....

LUNCH

....
....
....
....

DINNER

....
....
....
....

SNACK

....
....
....
....

NOTE

....
....
....
....

DAILY MEAL PLANNER

DAY 10

DATE:

BREAKFAST

....
....
....
....

LUNCH

....
....
....
....

DINNER

....
....
....
....

SNACK

....
....
....
....

NOTE

....
....
....
....

DAILY MEAL PLANNER

DAY 11

DATE:

BREAKFAST

....
....
....
....

LUNCH

....
....
....
....

DINNER

....
....
....
....

SNACK

....
....
....
....

NOTE

....
....
....
....

DAILY MEAL PLANNER

DAY 12

DATE:

BREAKFAST

....
....
....
....

LUNCH

....
....
....
....

DINNER

....
....
....
....

SNACK

....
....
....
....

NOTE

....
....
....
....

DAILY MEAL PLANNER

DAY 13

DATE:

BREAKFAST

....
....
....
....

LUNCH

....
....
....
....

DINNER

....
....
....
....

SNACK

....
....
....
....

NOTE

....
....
....
....

DAILY MEAL PLANNER

DAY 14

DATE:

BREAKFAST

....
....
....
....

LUNCH

....
....
....
....

DINNER

....
....
....
....

SNACK

....
....
....
....

NOTE

....
....
....
....